Date: 10/25/17

J 970.3 SEM
George, Gale,
Seminole /

SPOTLIGHT ON NATIVE AMERICANS

SEMINOLE

Gale George

PowerKiDS
press™

New York

Published in 2016 by The Rosen Publishing Group, Inc.
29 East 21st Street, New York, NY 10010

First Edition

Editor: Caitie McAneney
Book Design: Samantha DeMartin
Reviewed by: Robert J. Conley, Former Sequoyah Distinguished Professor at Western Carolina University and Director of Native American Studies at Morningside College and Montana State University. Supplemental material reviewed by: Donald A. Grinde, Jr., Professor of Transnational/American Studies at the State University of New York at Buffalo.

Photo Credits: Cover, p. 21 Marilyn Angel Wynn/Nativestock/Getty Images; pp. 5, 13 courtesy of Library of Congress; pp. 6–7 JTB Photo/Universal Images Group/Getty Images; p. 8 MPI/Archive Photos/Getty Images; pp. 9, 10–11 (main), 25, 29 Willard R. Culver/National Geographic/Getty Images; p. 10 (inset) Smithsonian American Art Museum/Wikimedia Commons; p. 12 Tripodero/ Wikimedia Commons; pp. 15, 17, 23 Otis Imboden/National Geographic/Getty Images; p. 19 Associated Press/AP Images; p. 22 Carlos Ginard/Flickr.com; p. 26 State Archives of Florida, Florida Memory/Wikimedia Commons; p. 27 Becky McCray/Flickr.com; p. 28 William F. Campbell/ The LIFE Images Collection/Getty Images.

Library of Congress Cataloging-in-Publication Data

George, Gale, author.
  Seminole / Gale George.
     pages cm. — (Spotlight on Native Americans)
  Includes index.
  ISBN 978-1-5081-4155-6 (pbk.)
  ISBN 978-1-5081-4156-3 (6 pack)
  ISBN 978-1-5081-4158-7 (library binding)
  1. Seminole Indians—History—Juvenile literature. 2. Seminole Indians—Social life and customs—Juvenile literature. I. Title.
  E99.S28G38 2016
  975.9004'973859—dc23
                         2015028137

Manufactured in the United States of America

CPSIA Compliance Information: Batch #BW16PK: For Further Information contact Rosen Publishing, New York, New York at 1-800-237-9932

CONTENTS

SEMINOLE ORIGINS

CHAPTER 1

The Seminole nation is one that's divided by distance, but united by **culture**. It's one of more than 500 Native American groups living throughout the United States. The Seminoles, who today live in Oklahoma and Florida, trace their origin back to the arrival of the very first people to America.

More than 12,000 years ago, ancestors of Native Americans traveled from Asia to North America. It was probably during a cold period called an **ice age**, when sea levels were much lower than they are now.

When the weather warmed again, the first peoples began to move, or migrate, around the Americas in small groups to find food. These small groups became separate peoples, and each one had a **unique** culture. Some learned to grow crops, allowing them to settle in one place permanently.

Pressure from European settlement in the 1700s forced the ancestors of the Seminoles to move south from Georgia and Alabama into Florida, which was controlled by the Spanish. Most of them were Creeks, also called

Muscogees, but other groups also migrated to northern Florida. Altogether, these peoples became known as the Seminoles around 1770.

Seminoles faced great unfairness from European settlers and the U.S. government over the course of centuries. They were forced from their land and sent to **reservations**, and their children were taken to boarding schools far away.

WHERE DID THE SEMINOLES COME FROM?

CHAPTER 2

Today, more than 8,000 Seminoles live on reservations in Florida and in the Seminole Nation reservation in Oklahoma. However, they have a rich history in other parts of North America. Their historic homelands include present-day Georgia and Alabama.

The Seminoles separated from the Muscogees in the 1700s. Both the Muscogees and Seminoles are descended from great civilizations of **Mound Builders** in the woodlands east of the Mississippi River. Today, state parks preserve some

of those historic earthen mounds. Many mounds are quite famous for their size. The base of the Monks Mound in Cahokia, Illinois, is even larger than the base of the Great Pyramid in Egypt!

The Seminoles and Muscogees also share a language family, which means many of their words are similar. The Muskogean language family is one of the greatest in the Southeast, and its languages are spoken by Muscogees, Choctaws, Chickasaws, and Seminoles. It's believed the Seminoles' name comes from a Spanish word meaning "wild." They have strong pride in their history.

Monks Mound

You can visit mounds around the country to learn more about the mound-building ancestors of the Seminole people.

MIGRATING TO FLORIDA

CHAPTER 3

Before the Seminoles arrived in Florida, other Native Americans were living there. However, like many groups, they were wiped out by European diseases and violence. During the 1700s, Muscogees from present-day Georgia and Alabama began moving to northern Florida for the empty land. By 1775, they had formed a separate tribe, known as the Seminoles.

In northern Florida, the Seminoles became successful farmers and ranchers, and other native groups joined them. Their growing population increased yet again when African American slaves began running away from the English and joining the Seminoles. The Seminoles still used these people as slaves, but they were treated better than they were by colonists. Some former slaves married Seminoles.

In the early 1800s, slave owners on the border of Florida and Georgia invaded Florida to recapture their runaway slaves. War broke out between the Seminoles and Georgians. In 1818, General Andrew Jackson sent the U.S. Army to attack the Seminoles. Spain sold Florida to the United States, and Americans began moving to Florida. Seminoles had to move further south. By the Second Seminole War, fought from 1835 to 1842, the Seminoles had been removed to the wetlands of central and southern Florida.

The Florida Everglades is a difficult region to farm. It's a huge area of tall grass growing out of shallow water with small, hidden islands. The Seminoles had to change their ways of farming and learn to hunt and fish in this new **environment**.

SEMINOLES FIGHT FOR THEIR LAND

CHAPTER 4

The Seminoles had moved to a new place, but soon, the United States demanded they leave. In 1830, the United States passed the Indian Removal Act and demanded that all Seminoles leave Florida. Some Seminoles signed the **Treaty** of Payne's Landing in 1832, and they were forced to move to Indian Territory, or what today is Oklahoma. This long and dangerous journey became known as the Trail of Tears.

Led by war chiefs Osceola and Wild Cat, some Seminoles decided to go to war instead of leaving. The war lasted from 1835 to 1842 and

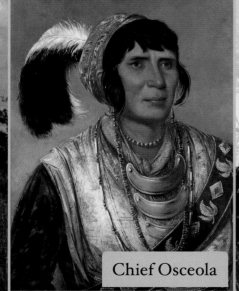

Chief Osceola

became the most expensive Native American war in U.S. history. Many Seminoles died, as did nearly 1,500 U.S. soldiers. Hundreds of Seminoles hid in the swamps until the army gave up trying to remove them. In 1855, another war broke out, and once again, the U.S. Army couldn't defeat the remaining Seminoles. This group of Seminole people remained in Florida.

Native Americans across eastern America were also removed from their land. Without enough food or supplies, many Native Americans died on their journey. By 1858, most Seminoles had been forced from their home to live in Indian Territory. They were forced to become part of the Muscogee Nation once again.

The Seminoles who avoided removal became a forgotten people. They survived mostly by hunting and fishing in southern Florida.

RESERVATION LIFE
CHAPTER 5

Once in Indian Territory, Seminoles were forced to live on reservations. Conditions in the Muscogee Nation were horrible. The U.S. government failed to supply the food and farming equipment it had promised. Additionally, the Seminoles suffered great hardship during the American Civil War, which lasted from 1861 to 1865.

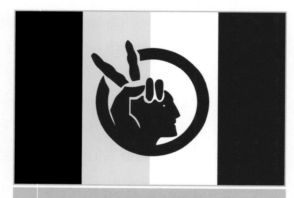

American Indian Movement Flag

The American Civil War was fought between the northern states, called the Union, and the southern states, called the Confederacy. During the war, both sides invaded Indian Territory to **raid** farms and steal food and livestock. The war divided the Seminole people because Seminole soldiers joined in the war on both sides.

It wasn't until after the war that the Seminoles in Indian Territory were allowed to form a nation separate from the

Muscogees. The Seminole Nation created a school system, and its members became prosperous farmers. Unfortunately, white settlers demanded the land for themselves in the 1870s and 1880s.

In 1907, the land the Seminoles lived on became part of the new state of Oklahoma. The Seminoles and other native peoples were forced to become citizens of the new state. They had to give up their land again, settling for small individual farms, and their nation was destroyed.

It wasn't until 1935 that the Seminoles in Oklahoma were allowed to form a limited government. In the midst of the American Indian Movement of the 1970s, the Seminoles were finally allowed to adopt a **constitution**. They formed their own government called the Seminole Nation of Oklahoma.

SEMINOLE CULTURE AND TRADITIONS

CHAPTER 6

The Seminole people faced plenty of hardship and separation, but through it all, they kept their culture and traditions alive. In Seminole culture, families are matrilineal. That means a person's family tree is traced through the mother's line, rather than the father's. Seminole culture is also matrilocal, which means that when a man and woman get married, they live with the wife's extended family. Their children are automatically members of the wife's **clan**.

In Seminole culture, uncles play a very important part in a child's life. Seminole children receive much of their training from their uncles, especially their mother's brothers. Parents are believed to be too emotionally close to their children to see what's best for them, so uncles have more responsibility in raising the child than the parents do.

The Seminoles survived by changing some ways of life to better fit the water-covered Everglades. For example, the environment made it more difficult to carry on their traditional government, which had been based on villages. In the swamps, people were more scattered and had to live in extended-family groups led by **elders**.

Seminoles in southern Florida traditionally lived in dwellings called chickees. This dwelling is built on a platform a few feet above the ground to protect it against flooding. A chickee has no walls so cool breezes can flow through the house.

SEMINOLE SKILLS

CHAPTER 7

A big reason Seminoles were able to adapt to new environments is because they're very skilled in building, crafting, and creating tools and clothing. The Seminoles in Florida were skilled in the art of building boats suited to the shallow waters of the Everglades. They'd fashion a tree log into a long, narrow, lightweight craft. A person would stand in the back of the boat and push it with a long pole. They made dugout canoes for traveling in ocean waters.

Seminole women developed styles of clothing that are among the most unique of all the Native Americans. They use patches of cloth, sewn together in strips of alternating color and pattern, to make colorful dresses and shirts. Grandmothers and mothers teach their craft to their daughters and granddaughters so the tradition lives on.

Seminoles are also skilled in sports and games. Like many Native Americans, Seminoles enjoy a game called "stickball," which inspired the modern sport of lacrosse. Big stickball games, called "match games," excited the entire tribe. Villages would compete against one another, and people would bet nearly all their possessions on one game.

Seminoles love playing stickball and other competitive sports. They also enjoy footraces and archery. They place great value on athletics, and there are sports teams for both men and women.

A STRONG BELIEF SYSTEM

CHAPTER 8

Seminoles have a strong belief system that has survived despite their hardships and attempts by the U.S. government to **assimilate** them. Traditional Seminoles try to live in harmony with the natural world. From the Seminole viewpoint, humans are merely one of the many creatures on Earth, and all creatures have a spirit that must be respected.

Many Seminole stories tell of lessons passed down by various animals about how to live in the world. It's impossible to understand how Seminoles view the world and their place in it without closely studying their stories and lessons.

Seminoles also believe in the power of medicine men. They believe medicine men have detailed knowledge of the healing powers of herbs and other remedies. Medicine men also carefully preserve the knowledge of magic potions and ceremonies that the people rely on to maintain their health and well-being. The most important religious event in Seminole culture is the Green Corn Ceremony. This event lasts four to seven days in late spring or early summer. Seminoles camp together, play games, and participate in ceremonies and rituals as well as dances and feasts.

This Seminole man is fixing the roof of his traditional home in the Florida Everglades.

SEMINOLE CREATION STORY

CHAPTER 9

The Seminoles' tale about their origin is a central part of their culture. According to the story, the Creator made Earth. He created and shaped many animals to live there. When he was satisfied that he had made enough creatures, the Creator put them all in a large shell next to a tree. The tree's roots wound around the shell and cracked it. Wind blew around the shell, giving the animals air to breathe and helping them to break free. The panther, which was once a common animal in southern Florida, was the Creator's favorite.

Once the animals were made, the Creator went about making people. He put people in a cave under the ground. Then, he made the ground shake and the cave burst open. Surrounded by fog, the people wandered around in small groups until the wind blew away the fog.

Each group was helped by one of the animals, which taught them how to survive. Each group took the name of its animal. Clans were named for deer, panthers, alligators, and more. Only eight clans have survived in Florida.

The people of the Panther Clan were favored by the Creator and became the medicine men and lawmakers.

TODAY'S FLORIDA SEMINOLES

CHAPTER 10

The Seminole Tribe of Florida is recognized as an independent group. Today, around 3,000 Seminoles live on six reservations in Florida. Big Cypress Reservation is the largest of the federal reservations at 52,480 acres (21,238 ha), and it's located on the northeastern edge of Big Cypress Swamp in southern Florida. The Brighton Reservation is 35,800 acres (14,488 ha), and it's located northwest of Lake Okeechobee. In 1962, the Miccosukees gained recognition by the U.S. government as a separate Native American group. They created several reservations in the Everglades, close to Big Cypress Reservation. The two main reservations are Tamiami Trail Reservation and Alligator Alley Reservation.

Each reservation in Florida has its own council to govern it. The councils come together each year at the Green Corn Ceremony. They look for business opportunities, including **casinos**, campgrounds, and the sale of tobacco. With profits from casinos, the Seminoles have built many houses, schools for their children, health-care facilities, community centers, and veterans' centers. They also make money through tourism in the Everglades and even alligator wrestling.

The Billie Swamp Safari in Big Cypress Reservation takes visitors on a swamp boat ride through the Everglades. They also have a museum that shows how the Seminoles used to live.

OKLAHOMA SEMINOLES

CHAPTER 11

The Seminole Nation of Oklahoma's capital is in Wewoka, Oklahoma. Over 5,000 Seminoles live there, and around 17,000 people are members of the nation. The Seminole Nation governs itself with an elected council made up of two members from each of the nation's 14 groups. They operate businesses, as well as provide educational programs for Seminole children, community centers, and health-care programs. They also encourage more people to learn the Seminole language. Their most important goal is to maintain **sovereignty**. They guard the Seminole nation from injustice from the U.S. government.

In the early 1900s, a great oil boom took place on Seminole land in Oklahoma. That should have made the Seminoles very wealthy. However, most were cheated out of their land by unjust politicians, lawyers, and judges. Now many Seminoles live near the **poverty** level.

Despite injustices, the Seminole Nation of Oklahoma has kept their culture strong. Craftspeople and artists sell their products at the Seminole Nation Museum in Wewoka. There,

Seminole women show their skill in making patchwork clothing. The Seminole Nation also holds a celebration of their culture each September. It highlights their arts and crafts, food, and dancing.

Patchwork clothing has become a traditional style of clothing for Seminoles. It began around the late 1800s, when there was a shortage of cloth. Seminole women sewed long, thin strips of different cloths together to make beautiful, colorful clothes.

FAMOUS SEMINOLES

CHAPTER 12

Throughout the past century, Seminoles have fought for more power and more opportunities for leadership. They've learned new ways to express their culture and history through writing and works of art. In fact, Seminoles have produced many famous artists and leaders.

Seminole journalist and Native American leader Betty Mae Tiger Jumper became the first woman elected to lead the council for the Seminole Nation of Florida in 1967. In 1949, she was the first Florida Seminole to graduate from high school. She founded a newspaper for the tribe in 1963 and became its editor. In 1997, she earned the Lifetime Achievement Award from the Native American Journalists Association.

Jerome Tiger was a Creek Seminole raised in Oklahoma,

Betty Mae Tiger Jumper

and he's considered one of the most famous Native American artists. His paintings illustrate events ranging from the Green Corn Ceremony to the Trail of Tears to modern Native American life. Another artist, sculptor Kelly Haney, was a leader in the Oklahoma Senate for many years. In 2002, one of Haney's sculptures of a Native American was placed on top of the dome of the Oklahoma State Capitol building.

Haney's sculpture

The Seminole contributions to art, journalism, and politics help others understand the greatness of the tribe and its strong history.

THE FUTURE OF THE SEMINOLES

CHAPTER 13

The Seminoles have come a long way to have their own land and govern themselves. They were forced to move from northern Florida to the Everglades, and then most were removed to Oklahoma. They were cheated out of land and money, and faced great poverty and injustice. Today, they have a new set of challenges.

Miccosukee Seminoles in Florida are worried about the worsening pollution of the Everglades swamps where they live. The main pollutants are chemicals used in farming that eventually enter the swamps. Buffalo Tiger, a former Miccosukee chief, was a leader in the

campaign to clean up the swamps. He said, "We lived off the Everglades, and we can't do that now. But if things keep going like this, when our young people grow up, they won't have anything left."

While Seminoles still face injustices and hardship, from corruption to pollution to poverty, they've been able to keep their culture alive. Today, many hold leadership positions not only in the tribe, but in their separate professions. The Seminoles are a patchwork culture. They may be separated by distance, but they're woven together by their strong history.

The Seminoles were able to survive because they could adapt to new environments and conditions. Their culture is one that will surely not be lost.

GLOSSARY

assimilate: To cause a person or group to become part of a different society or country.

casino: A building or room used for gambling.

clan: A group of related families.

constitution: The basic laws by which a country, state, or group is governed.

culture: The beliefs and ways of life of a group of people.

elder: One who has authority because of their age and experience.

environment: The conditions that surround a living thing and affect the way it lives.

ice age: A period during which temperatures fall worldwide and large areas are covered with glaciers.

Mound Builder: A member of a prehistoric Native American people who built huge earthen mounds from the Great Lakes down the Mississippi River valley to the Gulf of Mexico.

poverty: The state of being poor.

raid: To carry out a sudden attack.

reservation: Land set aside by the government for a specific Native American group or groups to live on.

sovereignty: Independence.

treaty: An agreement among nations or peoples.

unique: One of a kind.

FOR MORE INFORMATION

BOOKS

Gibson, Karen Bush. *Native American History for Kids: With 21 Activities*. Chicago, IL: Chicago Review Press, 2010.

Sanford, William R. *Seminole Chief Osceola*. Berkeley Heights, NJ: Enslow Publishers, 2013.

Wilcox, Charlotte. *The Seminoles*. Minneapolis, MN: Lerner Publications, 2007.

WEBSITES

Due to the changing nature of Internet links, PowerKids Press has developed an online list of websites related to the subject of this book. This site is updated regularly. Please use this link to access the list: www.powerkidslinks.com/sona/semi

INDEX